Starting Over

....

How Not to Screw Up
Your Next Relationship

William P. Smith

New
Growth
Press
www.newgrowthpress.com

New Growth Press, Greensboro, NC 27429
Copyright © 2009 by Christian Counseling & Educational Foundation
All rights reserved. Published 2009.

Typesetting: Robin Black, www.blackbirdcreative.biz

ISBN-10: 1-935273-01-9
ISBN-13: 978-1-935273-01-1

Library of Congress Cataloging-in-Publication Data

Smith, William P., 1965-
 Starting over : how not to screw up your next relationship /
William P. Smith.
    p. cm.
Includes bibliographical references and index.
ISBN-13: 978-1-935273-01-1 (alk. paper)
ISBN-10: 1-935273-01-9 (alk. paper)
 1. Man-woman relationships—Religious aspects—
Christianity. 2. Dating (Social customs)—Religious aspects—
Christianity. I. Title.
BT705.8.S65 2009
248.8′4—dc22

                                        2009016565

Printed in Canada

11 12 13   4 5 6

So, your last relationship went sour. Maybe it was so fast and furious, with so much light and heat, that it burned itself out. Maybe you were engaged when one or both of you decided it wasn't going to work. Or, hardest of all, perhaps you were married when, sadly, everything fell apart.

Whatever happened, you are single again, and you've been thinking about or toying with the idea of getting involved with someone new. You might be attracted to someone right now, or perhaps you're just thinking about the possibility for the future.

You're a little nervous—you'd like to have a new relationship—but you're not sure, given your track record, how good an idea that is. Certainly the other person in your previous relationship had his or her share of issues, but in your more thoughtful moments you know you also had yours.

Because you've got issues to address, you've also got questions: Should you start something with someone else? Will you be toxic or nurturing this time? What were you supposed to learn from your past experience(s)? How do you know you're ready to try again?

While no one can tell you exactly what to do, this booklet will help you think through your questions from God's perspective.

Do You Have More Confidence in God's Redemption or in Your Failure?

Four months after his fiancé broke their engagement, Todd said, "This was all part of the plan." For some people that would be a depressing statement of resignation. But Todd didn't see himself as a helpless victim of fate.

Instead, despite the many mistakes he had made in his relationship with his fiancé, he saw a very personal, active, powerful God redeeming those mistakes—in both of their lives. When Todd spoke of "the plan" he spoke with confidence in God's promise to use even Todd's failures for his good. He believed what God said: "'For I know the plans I have for you,' declares the LORD, 'plans to prosper you and not to harm you, plans to give you hope and a future'" (Jeremiah 29:11). And he believed that God was using all things in his life for his good (Romans 8:28).

Do you have a deep-seated confidence that Jesus' mercy to you and his plans for you go deeper than your failings? People who are ready to move on to a new relationship know that their errors and missteps haven't relegated them to plan B (or C, D, E . . . Z for that matter!). They know that, in some mysterious way, God wraps their mistakes back into his good purposes for them.

If you're still struggling to believe that God will redeem your worst relational failures, then you're not ready to move on. You need to know what good things God has brought out of your failed relationship before embarking on a new one.

Trusting Jesus, Loving Others

When a relationship falls apart, you may struggle with whether you can really trust another person again.

Maybe you learned some things about the other person that surprised you. Maybe he hid parts of himself from you or maybe you chose not to see who she really was. Either way, the reality feels the same—you've seen the darker side of humanity, and now you're not sure if you can give yourself to someone else after being so disappointed.

You've learned the hard way what Jesus already knew. The apostle John said that Jesus didn't entrust himself to people, because he knew what was inside of them (John 2:23–25). Yet, Jesus stands out as the most intensely relational person in the whole Bible. He enjoyed people, spent time with them, helped them, rebuked them, cared for them, served them, and wept for them. His knowledge of our true nature didn't hold him back from relating deeply with the people around him.

His entire ministry revolved around removing the obstacles to relationship with him. His life, death, and resurrection made a way for us to spend eternity with him. And so we look forward to the day when the new Jerusalem will come down from heaven, and we will hear, "Now the dwelling of God is with men, and he will live with them. They will be his people, and God himself will be with them and be their God" (Revelation 21:3).

Your friendship with Jesus is the best friendship you will ever have. Other friends might prove to be untrustworthy, but Jesus will never fail you. You can depend on his love and friendship. Trusting Jesus frees you to love, serve, help, and enjoy sinful humans without losing yourself in them or being walked on by them. One of the best things you can learn in the aftermath of a failed relationship is to trust Jesus' unfailing love and ask him to help you love others as he has loved you.

Relearn the Gospel

As you spend time reflecting on God's love for you and his good plan for your life, it is also very important to think seriously about your own relational failings. How you relate to others always reflects the state of your faith in God. Because faith expresses itself in love (Galatians 5:6), every failure to love is simultaneously a failure to live by faith.

Let's flesh this out with two simple examples:

1. When you are relationally pushy (aggressive, controlling, nagging, forceful, demanding), you don't believe that God is big enough or interested enough to put things right in your relationship. So when someone upsets you or hurts you, you fill in the gap. You act on your (false) confidence that God is not going to do anything by pressuring your friend to change—NOW. You have greater faith in your ability to produce the change *you* want in your friend than in God's ability to produce the change *he* wants.

2. When you are relationally passive (retreating, disengaged, apathetic, not trying, ignoring others), then you functionally believe that God can't fix the mess you've made. You think that

God can't act—or won't!—and since nothing you do seems to make a difference, you grow discouraged and stop moving toward others.

Those two false faiths—that God is unable or unwilling to act—keep you from loving well. The apostle Paul clearly explains real love by saying, "Love is patient, love is kind. It does not envy, it does not boast, it is not proud. It is not rude, it is not self-seeking, it is not easily angered, it keeps no record of wrongs. Love does not delight in evil but rejoices with the truth. It always protects, always trusts, always hopes, always perseveres" (1 Corinthians 13:4–7). When you see yourself doing the opposite of what Paul calls us to do—when instead of loving others you are impatient, unkind, envious, boastful, proud, rude, self-seeking, easily angered, and unable to forgive—then you can be sure that your belief and your experience of Christ's goodness and power is weak.

Until you've seen, confessed, and repented of your lack of confidence in Jesus' power to transform your relationships, you're not ready to move on. However, when you do see yourself relying on Jesus to move in love toward others (instead of pressuring or retreating), then you might be ready to consider a more serious relationship. So take a moment now and go to him. Tell him the ways that you failed in your relationship. Ask him to forgive you for how you didn't trust him and love others. Remember that because of Jesus' death for you, God always stands ready to forgive (1 John 1:8–9).

Self-Assessment

Knowing that God is always ready to forgive you will give you the courage to honestly assess yourself. It is easy to think that just changing the things around you—your job, your home, your school—will make things better. If you apply this to your relationships (and many do), then the solution to your relationship problems seems simple—just change your partner.

The problem with this strategy is that you will still be you, and you will take you with you wherever you go. You carry both your good and bad relational qualities into every new friendship. That means you need to take the time to examine this part of your life. As you think about the reasons your previous relationship failed, you'll notice the places where you need to grow.

The writer of Psalm 139 wanted to understand himself better, so he invited the Lord to search him and know his heart to see if there was any offensive way in him (vv. 23–24). He confidently appealed to God because he realized that nothing was hidden from him; God not only knew what the psalmist did, but also what he thought. In fact, there was nowhere in all of creation he could go without God already being there.

But this all-seeing, everywhere God doesn't need a human invitation to know his creatures—he already does know them! That's when you realize that the psalmist is asking to know for himself what God knows about him. He's asking to see himself through the eyes of God.

That kind of bold request might frighten you. Some people would prefer to do almost anything except assess themselves because they expect that they would be overwhelmed, disappointed, or even repulsed by what they see. When Ryan came for counsel, he said that between his home stereo, car radio, and portable mp3 player, he plays music constantly so he is never alone with his thoughts for more than thirty seconds at a time.

That strategy only makes sense when you're not sure how much Jesus loves you. It is scary to look at yourself if you think that your relationship with him depends on how good you are. But let this truth sink in deeper than your fears: *his* goodness brought you into his family and, now that you belong, *his* goodness is what keeps you in. The safety and security that he gives you is what lets you look at yourself, invite his perspective, and ask (as well as answer!) the hard questions.

Your relationships can be different not because you change your partner, but because Jesus—your most enduring, changeless partner—changes you.

If you haven't identified or worked to reverse poor relational habits, then you're not ready to move on. As you rely on Christ to change how you relate to your present friends, you can be confident that he will also help you in a more romantic relationship.

Others' Assessment

When you've been burned relationally—it doesn't matter by whom or how severely—your natural inclination is to pull away from people. But retreating is dangerous because we were created to live in communities—to actively and regularly share our lives with each other. Without active interaction, we forfeit some of our humanity.

Part of being human means you share your heart and life with those who care for you, and you listen to their input. If your family, friends, and pastors believe you're ready to try a more intense relationship, you should be encouraged to go forward. If they recommend that waiting a bit longer will be good for you, then you should slow down.

There are two things to avoid as you listen to the advice of others: letting others make your decisions for you; or only listening to the advice you want to hear. Despite those dangers, you still need your community to help you decide if you are ready to enter into a deeper relationship. The Book of Proverbs tells us that the wise person listens to the advice of others (Proverbs 12:15; 15:22). If you are closed off to any voice except your own, then you're not ready to move on. But you're also not ready if other voices mean too much to you. If you're already seeking and carefully assessing other people's input, then take heart! You're handling relationships in a healthy, mature manner right now.

How Long Will It Take?

After reading this, you might think you will never be ready for a new relationship! But put your hope in God, not yourself, and ask him to change you so you can grow in love for him and for others. That doesn't guarantee that your next relationship will be a keeper, but it does guarantee something much more important—that you are becoming more like Jesus.

Practical Strategies for Change

Here are some things you can do that will help you to practically apply the ideas in the previous section:

1. Start by making a list of what you've learned from your past failed relationships. How has your confidence in God's good power grown or shrunk? Spend some time in prayer thanking him for what he's taught you.

2. Make a list of the ways you've failed to love. What roots of false faith led to your non-love? Repent of your lack of faith in Christ, and ask him to give you a heart that can really love others. Take a psalm of repentance and pray through it, such as Psalm 32, 51, or 130.

3. Take the time to examine your present reasons for wanting to meet someone new. Are you focused on what *you* will get—a sense of being super-special; an intense feeling of belonging; someone to point to when your grandma asks if you're seeing anyone? If you're looking to be filled, more than you're looking to love, then you're probably not yet ready to be romantically involved.

4. Include the body of Christ. Share your lists and thoughts with a friend or family member and someone from your church's pastoral staff. Ask for their thoughts on what you've shared and get their sense of your readiness.

Don't try to address everything on your lists at one time. Read through this booklet again and pick just one area in your life that you would like to see changed. Perhaps you need to grow in your confidence in God's loving control over your life, or maybe you need to grow in your love for others. Whatever it is, ask God for the desire to work on this issue and also ask a few friends to pray for you. Then apply what you are learning in the context of your current non-romantic friendships. Every few months pick up your lists and see what new things God has taught you about trusting him and loving others.

Meeting New People

When you feel like you are ready to start a new relationship, it's natural to wonder where exactly you can go or what you can do to meet someone new. But, if your goal is simply to trust Jesus and love others, then there will be no shortage of people to be in relationship with. If you look around your church, your work, and your neighborhood, you'll see lots of people who need love and care. Since there are more than six billion people on our planet, there will always be plenty of opportunities for you to love.

As a human you absolutely need to be relationally attached (it is *not* good for you to be alone), but—and this is important—what you need is attachment and connection, not necessarily romance. So look around where you are and build relationships.

Small groups at your church are a place where relationships often begin. Having a scheduled time and activity provides an opportunity for a structured connection with others. You can add more time and activity outside of the group as your friendship grows.

Or you can invite people over to share a meal with you. As a single person, I learned to be bold and regularly invited myself over to other people's houses for dinner (it is much easier for a single to go to a family's house than vice versa—just make sure you ask what you can bring!).

At other times when I've found myself low on the friend-meter, I've asked people I wanted to get to know if they would consider going out for breakfast before work. Other people get together for coffee at night.

You'll think of your own variations for how to spend time with people. The important point is to develop your ability to build connections with other people.

Romantic relationships are never less than really good regular relationships. So share your life now with those around you, and if, in God's providence, he allows you to develop a romantic interest, you'll be that much more ready and that much less needy. Growing in your trust of God's care for you and your relationships will give you the freedom to love those whom God puts in your life, without worrying about finding your next romantic interest. God will provide every relationship you need at just the right time.

If you were helped by reading this booklet, perhaps you or someone you know would also be encouraged by these booklets: